C000165696

THE SOUTHERN RAILWAY
VICTORIA STATION
a unique perspective

Bruce Murray & Kevin Robertson

VICTORIA STATION

a unique perspective

The genus for this book came about purely by chance. That chance began at an exhibition in June 2007 where Solent Railway Auctions had a display advertising their forthcoming June Railwayana auction. Amongst the items brought along to tempt potential bidders was a small black photographic album headed "Victoria Station, Plan and Photographs of Premises - 'On Appeal'." Its interest was immediate and we were fortunately successful in securing the album at auction shortly afterwards.

The book itself contains just over 40 photographs and plans and although undated, a quick piece of research reveals it to relate to an appeal by the Southern Railway against Westminster City Council to the House of Lords in 1936.

Further research reveals the Southern had at the time commenced to sub-let sites on their stations, Victoria being the first. This was for outside commercial purposes and naturally then charged the various businesses rent. This action the railway considered was within their own remit, as they were already paying rent themselves for the actual station site. Westminster Council however had a different view and successfully prosecuted the railway in the lower courts before the whole matter wound up on appeal to the Law Lords.

The Southern Railway won, and which in turn led to the rapid expansion of private enterprise onto railway premises resulting eventually in the situation we have decades later where a station concourse could perhaps even be said to resemble a shopping arcade. Indeed the legal case won by the Southern Railway is still quoted years later as precedent for similar actions.

In connection with the original legal case and thus to assist in their deliberations, the Law Lords had produced a set of photographs showing the contemporary Victoria Station complete with the various business outlets then under debate. Whilst the caption information accompanying these is very limited, curiously certain railway facilitates such as the booking office are also included. Additionally from some small sketch plans, one example of which is included in the following pages, it would appear that certain rooms and facilities below platform level and also on the first and second floors of the station office block had been similarly sub-let and were therefore likewise subject to the same appeal. These areas though were not photographed. Likewise the album occasionally contains the reference 'Not under appeal'.

This then is the subject of this book. A unique look back at the commence of a major London Termini, and one we believe to have been singly recorded in this way. Certainly the detail does not appear for any other location at the time, or even since.

The photographs are so beautifully clear and detailed we took the decision to deliberately limit the amount of additional material that would be added, using instead just the original few words from the album.. Accordingly this is not a book intended for the locomotive or multiple unit devotee, but instead one for the connoisseur who values a true record of a past era. The few additional views we have added have been specially selected so as to be in keeping with the original work. The amazing detail within the original album also means we can take the opportunity to enlarge specific areas on some of the photographs and so obtain the benefit of maximum detail.

We sincerely hope you enjoy the results as much as we have taken please in its compilation.   Bruce Murray and Kevin Robertson

GENERAL VIEW - EAST SIDE

GENERAL VIEW - WEST SIDE

BAGGAGE
& REGISTRATION
OFFICE.

INSURE
YOUR
BAGGAGE
HERE.

NEWS THEATRE
NOW OPEN AT THIS STATION
ENTRANCE ADJOINING PLATFORM Nº 17.

INSURE
YOUR
BAGGAGE
HERE.

INSURE
YOUR
BAGGAGE
HERE.

IN

OUT

*EAST SIDE BOOKING
HALL. PART OF KIOSK*

EAST SIDE BOOKING HALL, KIOSK (TOBACONNISTS).
FREDERICK HOTELS Ltd. PART OF KIOSK

EAST SIDE, NEAR BOOKING HALL, BOOKSTALL.
W H SMITH & Son Ltd.

Who is **NEVRIL?**
The man who takes **BOVRIL**

HERNE BAY GOLF CLUB
18 HOLES
5 MINUTES WALK FROM HERNE BAY STATION

Great ICE HOCKEY Match
FRANCE ENGLAND
NOVEMBER 21ST
IMPERIAL ICE-RINK PURLEY

Fuller's

EAST SIDE, ON CONCOURSE, KIOSK (CONFECTIONERS).
FULLERS Ltd.

EAST SIDE, ON CONCOURSE, KIOSK (CONFECTIONERS).
FREDERICK HOTELS Ltd.

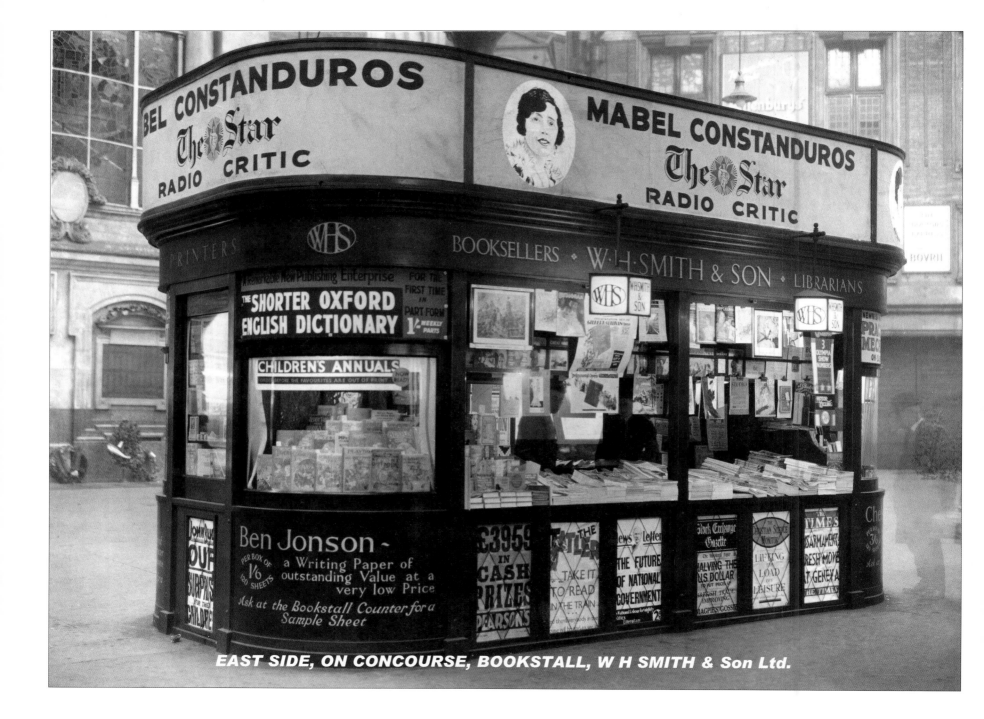

EAST SIDE, ON CONCOURSE, BOOKSTALL, W H SMITH & Son Ltd.

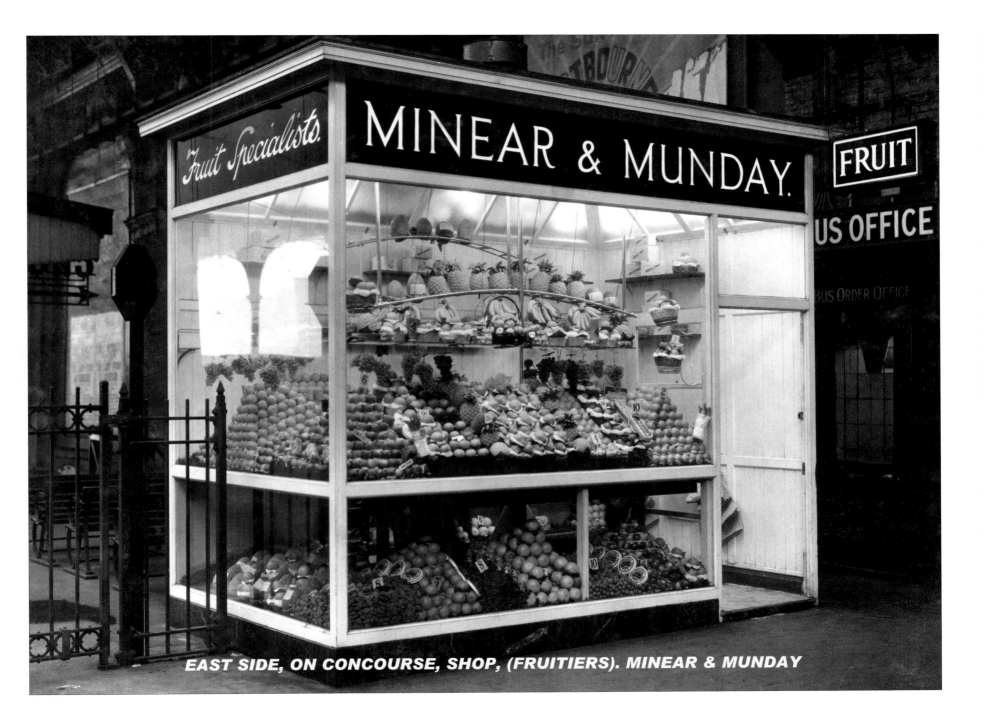

EAST SIDE, ON CONCOURSE, SHOP, (FRUITIERS). MINEAR & MUNDAY

BUS OFFICE

RICKARDS OMNIBUS OFFICE

PLATFORM No. 11 FOR BANSTEAD AND NORK PARK ESTATE

APPLY
THE BUILDERS
PERRYS (EALING) L^d
Estate Office. Banstead S^t

MOTOR BUSES.   MOTOR CARS.   MOTOR VANS.

EAST SIDE, ON CONCOURSE, BUS OFFICE, CHARLES RICHARDS Ltd.

EAST SIDE, ON CONCOURSE, BANK, NATIONAL PROVINCIAL BANK Ltd.

CONFECTIONERY   TOBAC

Agents for *Fuller's* CONFECTIONERY

E. HERBERT & CO. LTD.   TOBACCO

TELEPHONE

29

CADBURY'S CHOCOLATES
SOLD HERE

Take This Opportunity
Large Stock of Genuine
**76 ANCHOR
BRIARS**
Must be Cleared
at **5 6**
This Offer Cannot be Repeated

Cadbury's Biscuits   Cadbury's Biscuits

PETER'S

NESTLÉ'S   NESTLÉ'S

KENSITAS

LEFT: EAST SIDE, ON CONCOURSE, KIOSK, (CONFECTIONERS).
HERBERT & Co Ltd.

RIGHT: EAST SIDE, ON CONCOURSE, KIOSK, (CONFECTIONERS).
FREDERICK HOTELS Ltd.

LOWER: WEST SIDE, BY ENTRANCE AND FACING STATION YARD, KIOSK, (TOBACCONISTS).
GORDON HOTELS Ltd.

EAST SIDE, WILTON ROAD. SIX SHOPS (STATION YARD SIDE).
Not under appeal.

EAST SIDE, WILTON ROAD. SIX SHOPS (WILTON ROAD SIDE).
Not under appeal.

STATION YARD 'BUS STATION.
LONDON PASSENGER TRANSPORT BOARD.
Not under appeal.

EDWᴰ HERBERT & Cᵒ Lᵀᴰ

REGᴰ OFFICES. 7 PLOUGH YARD E.C.2

CONFECTIONERY

CREMINS de FER de L'OUEST

Rouen

WEST SIDE, FACING STATION YARD, SHOP (CONFECTIONERS).
HERBERT & Co Ltd. Not under appeal.

WEST SIDE, ON CONCOURSE, KIOSK
(TOBACCONISTS).
GORDON HOTELS Ltd.

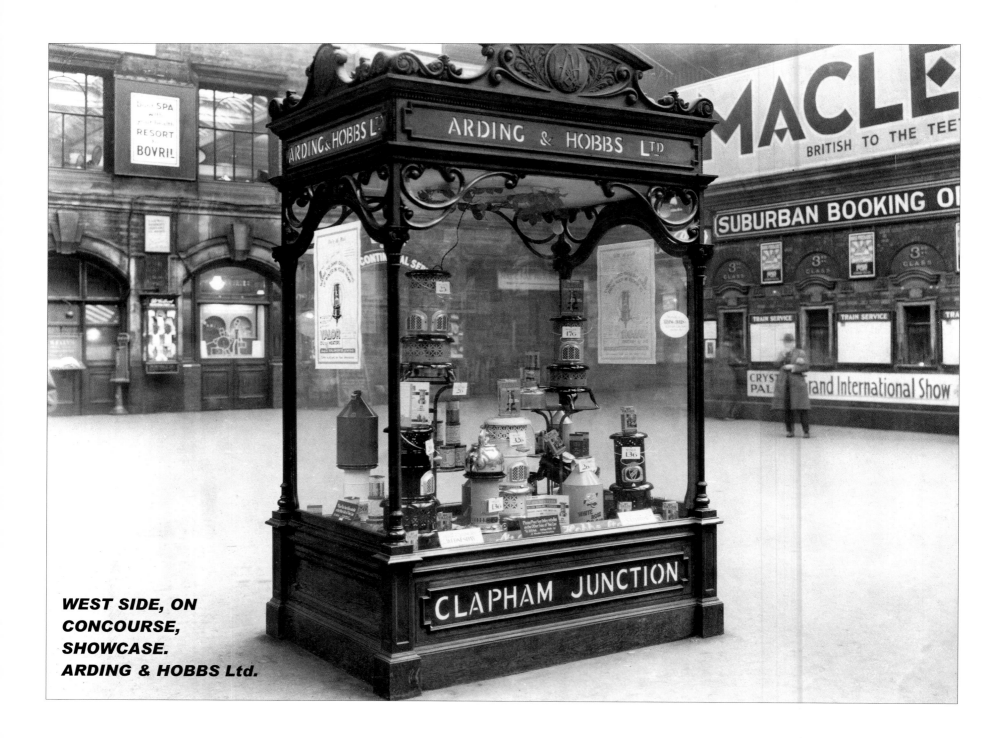

WEST SIDE, ON
CONCOURSE,
SHOWCASE.
ARDING & HOBBS Ltd.

WEST SIDE, ON CONCOURSE, SHOWCASE. J HARPER & Co Ltd.

**WEST SIDE, ON CONCOURSE, BOOKSTALL (former structure).
W H SMITH & Son Ltd.**

WEST SIDE, ON CONCOURSE, BOOKSTALL (new structure).
W H SMITH & Son Ltd.

CONFECTIONERY

WEST SIDE, ON CONCOURSE, KIOSK (CONFECTIONERS).
GORDON HOTELS Ltd.

WEST SIDE, MAIN BOOKING HALL, SHOP (FRUITIERS).
MILNEAR & MUNDAY

**WEST SIDE, MAIN BOOKING HALL, SHOP (FLORISTS)
(FROM STATION YARD) M BROWN**

**WEST SIDE, MAIN BOOKING HALL, SHOP (FLORISTS)
(FROM BOOKING HALL) M BROWN**

WEST SIDE, MAIN BOOKING HALL, OFFICE (TOURIST AGENTS)
THOS. COOK & Son Ltd.

EXAMPLE OF THE ACCOMPANYING PLANS. THIS ONE CLEARLY REFERS TO FACILITIES BELOW PLATFORM LEVEL AND WAS PROBABLY INCLUDED AS PHOTOGRAPHS WERE NOT TAKEN.

28

SCALE   20 FEET TO 1 INCH

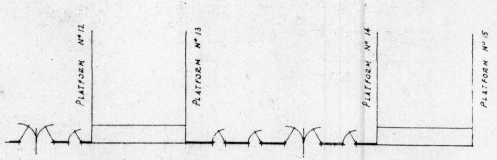

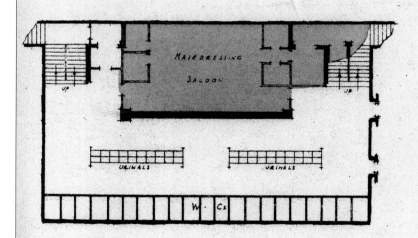

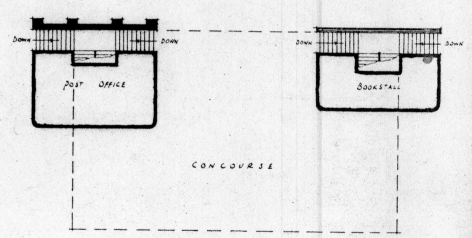

PLAN OF HAIRDRESSING SALOON & LAVATORY
UNDER CONCOURSE

PLAN OF ACCESS
FROM CONCOURSE

Nº IN SCHEDULE	SITUATION	DESCRIPTION	NAME	INCLUDED IN OR EXCLUDED FROM ROLL	COLOUR ON STATION PLAN
28	WEST SIDE. UNDER CONCOURSE	HAIRDRESSING SALOON IN GENTLEMEN'S LAVATORIES	F. R. PICKARD	INCLUDED	RED

WEST SIDE, ON CONCOURSE. BOOKSTALL (FORMER STRUCTURE).

W H SMITH & Son Ltd.

WEST SIDE, ON CONCOURSE. BOOKSTALL (NEW STRUCTURE).
W H SMITH & Son Ltd.

WEST SIDE, ON CONCOURSE (NEAR BOOKING HALL)
KIOSK, (TOBACCONISTS). GORDON HOTELS Ltd.

WEST SIDE, MAIN BOOKING HALL, SHOW WINDOW. BON MARCHE Ltd.

WEST SIDE, MAIN BOOKING HALL, SHOP (CARPETS AND JEWELLERY).
J SASSOON

WEST SIDE, ON CONCOURSE, SHOP AND BASEMENT (CHEMISTS).
BOOTS CASH CHEMISTS (SOUTHERN) Ltd.

WEST SIDE, ON
CONCOURSE,
KIOSK
(CONFECTIONERS).
HERBERT & Co Ltd.

WEST SIDE, ON CONOURSE, SHOWCASE. PARNELLS Ltd.

**WEST SIDE, ABOVE PARCELS OFFICE, ADJOINING No 15 PLATFORM.
HAIRDRESSING SALOON IN LADIES' LAVATORIES. Mrs E MYERS.**

10501

EAST CROYDON
REDHILL
HAYWARDS HEATH
BRIGHTON

GUARD   LUCCAGE

Loco I Tm.

OLD PASSENGER GALLERY, OFFICE. POSTMASTER GENERAL.

WEST SIDE, UNDER RAMP LEADING TO CAB RANK. CANTEEN. R COLLIS.

INSIDE COMPANY'S GATES BY TURNTABLE, BUCKINGHAM PALACE ROAD.
MOTOR GARAGE. O G C Drury

EXTENDING OVER ENTRANCE TO STATION, BUCKINGHAM PALACE ROAD.
NEWS THEATRE (FROM OUTSIDE STATION). BRTISH NEWS THEATRE Ltd.

EXTENDING OVER ENTRANCE TO STATION, BUCKINGHAM PALACE ROAD. NEWS THEATRE (FROM INSIDE STATION). BRTISH NEWS THEATRE Ltd.

WEST SIDE - NEW BOOKSTALL (VIEW FROM PLATFORM 15).

WEST SIDE - NEW BOOKSTALL (VIEW FROM CONCOURSE).

Although not part of the original album, the final three sides are contemporary with the subject in question. For this reason we have deliberately avoided captions to allow the photographs to speak for themselves.

BRIDGE PLACE, OLD GENERATING STATION (AS STORES).
PULLMAN CAR Co. Ltd.

NEWSAGENTS
ALSO MEDITERRANEAN
ASK FOR FOLDERS Head Office: 3 FENCHURCH ST. LONDON, E.C.3.
THE LARGEST COVERED SEA-WATER SWIMMING POOL IN THE WORLD
WEST STREET BRIGHTON
CHEAP TICKETS DAY THIS STATION
PHONE
TEMPLE BAR 3161
EVERY EVENING
6.30 & 9.0
MATINEE 2.30 SATURDAY
SKATE THOSE BLUES AWAY
PURLEY
THE COUNT OF MONTE CRISTO
SWAN VESTAS
NEWS THEATRE
JOHN BULL
City of London Gazette
LONDON'S GREAT DISPLAY AT B.I.F.
TO NEW YORK FOR £10
ELECTRICAL REVIEW
HEATING SOIL ELECTRICALLY
HOW TO BUY COAL
The One-lamp Consumer
LONDON ELECTRICITY MERGER
ANTI-VIVISECTION JOURNAL
THE LEADING PAPER ON THIS QUESTION

WEST SIDE - NEW BOOKSTALL (VIEW FROM PLATFORM 15).

'Evening time at Victoria', a fitting conclusion.
Howard Butler Collection.